Delta Pine Summer

by Beth Wiggins

Foreword

It was a world and a time of its own, the mid 1960's on Delta Pine Plantation in the Mississippi Delta. Cookouts at Uncle Joe's Landing, making witches brew with our bare feet on the sandbars of the mighty Mississippi River, rowing on Deer Creek while knocking copperheads off a wooden boat, earning a silver dollar for swimming the length of the swimming pool, fishing at Catfish Point – those poignant memories filled long Delta days in an era that is no more, a **Delta Pine Summer**.

Dedicated to Mama and Daddy

who interwove the magical amidst the mundane.

Table of Contents

Delta Pine Summer i
by Beth Wiggins i
Table of Contents iii
Milky Way Messengers 1
At Home on Deer Creek 3
Old Man River 6
The Lord's Day 11
Silver Dollar Incentive 16
Depot Downtown 19
Westward Bound 24
Grandma's Pink House 28
Fourth of July 32
Field Days 36
Summer's End 40

Milky Way Messengers

    The first firefly that flickered in the backyard marked the official beginning of a Mississippi Delta Summer. Like a sentinel from the Milky Way, he beamed Morse code in a series of on/off light flashes. Compelled, Margot and I chased him under pink-fluff mimosas and scent draped magnolia trees as he wound his way along the banks of nearby Deer Creek. As mysteriously as the creature had appeared, the firefly skillfully disappeared amid the stately cypress trees, night guardians of the creek bank, and vanished into the fragrant night air.

    The debut of the firefly ushered in the joyful transition called Summer. On the Delta and Pine Land Plantation, Summer meant cookouts at Uncle Joe's Landing, making witches brew with bare feet on the sand bars of the Mississippi River, sitting on the grassy top of the levee and finding the Big Dipper and the North Star. Summer meant Field Days at Delta Pine, home churned vanilla ice cream, fried okra, garden ripe tomatoes, and a host of delightful unplanned surprises.

    A few nights after the arrival of the fireflies, Margot and I each found a glass Mason jar in Mama's canning stores in the pantry. After poking holes in the lids with an ice pick, we raced about the backyard capturing as many of the elusive fireflies as our small hands could grasp.

    "Oooh, these fireflies tickle my palms," I grimaced to my older sister, Margot, and lost a few as the prisoners squirmed to break free. "It's like we're grabbing grasshoppers out of Daddy's wire mesh bait bucket to string on our fish hooks, only not quite so bad."

At bedtime we carefully placed the two Mason jars of fireflies on the dresser near our bunk beds and watched the tiny creatures blink signals. "Margot," I whispered. "I think these creatures are really Martians radioing their home planet in preparation for an invasion of Earth."

"You are nuts, Anna Beth," Margot retorted. "Besides, that scares me."

We tried to force our weary eyes to remain open, hoping to observe a midnight Martian spaceship rescue. But, the steady drone of the huge attic fan, the music of the katydids floating through open windows, and the distant horn of a lonely tug boat pushing its heavy load wearily down the Mississippi River lulled us into a deep summer night's slumber.

At Home on Deer Creek

I lived with my family of seven in the heart of the Mississippi Delta on the banks of Deer Creek. It was a quiet murky creek, bordered on each side by granddaddy cypress trees and knobby kneed cypress offspring, clumped together like families at a crowded mid-summer family reunion. Turtles sunbathed sleepily on cottonwood logs while cottonmouth snakes slithered like guilty convicts escaped from Parchman Prison, occasionally poking their black noses above water toward the sunlight. Often, we Delta Pine children paddled in the creek in an old wooden rowboat, stopping occasionally to knock a cottonmouth off the edge of the boat with broken wooden paddles. Deer Creek flowed lazily into nearby Lake Bolivar, hardly a stone's throw from the mighty Mississippi River.

Included in our household of seven were Daddy and Mama, then Margot, myself – Anna Beth, Stephan, Katy, and Dani. We children were like stair steps, all close in age. Our home was a white frame cottage with a large, screened front porch, the third to the last in a single row of quiet, well-kept houses with spacious yards facing Deer Creek.

Surrounding the house were wonderful trees for climbing – a large magnolia on the right side whose lower branches touched the ground and whose limbs we skillfully scaled to its very top. A mimosa tree and numerous shrubs to the left provided ample space for tea and coffee parties. A sycamore out front caught the street lamp night light, its crisp leaves flickering in the moonlight like silver pennies. In the back stood a huge cedar and some pecan trees where Daddy had hung a tire swing with a long rope and built a wooden playhouse.

Daddy's garden plot next to the playhouse boasted tall stalks of ripening sweet corn, bamboo poles wrapped with pole beans, rows of black-eyes peas, okra, butter beans, yellow squash, tomatoes, watermelon, and cantaloupe. Behind the house stretched acres of Delta Pine cotton fields growing green and strong in rich Delta soil at summer's onset.

Margot and I gathered magnolia cones with their red berries, acorns and their caps, sweet gum balls, pecans left by the squirrels from the previous season, cedar balls, and pink mimosa flowers for our pretend food stores. Assembling piles of sticks, magnolia leaves, and domed mushrooms, our world became a magical tea party in a mythical world of whimsical elves and fairies.

Mama brought out snacks on a tray – homemade peanut butter cookies flattened with the tines of a fork and still hot from the oven or snickerdoodle cookies thickly coated with cinnamon and sugar. Sometimes the snacks were homemade popsicles frozen in Tupperware popsicle molds. There was always sugared iced tea or Kool-Aid poured into tall plastic Tupperware glasses. Mama spread a patchwork quilt for all of us to pile on as we devoured our snacks. We rolled to our backs to watch the wind knead the clouds into animal shapes with caricature faces. Summer brought magic -- soft days honeycombed with sunshine, memories poignant as the fragrant southern breeze.

Old Man River

"Load up!" Daddy barked in his clipped military command voice. He had spent several years as an artillery officer at Fort Sill and Fort Bragg after finishing ROTC in undergraduate school. We piled into the bed of Daddy's truck amidst picnic supplies, guns, and buckets for blackberries. Charlie, our tri-colored beagle and Daddy's favorite hunting dog, hopped in and sat with paws on the side of the truck, panting in anticipation of the outing.

Slowly we traveled the familiar five miles of graveled road past lush pasture land with grazing beef cattle, near wooded hamlets laden with wild pecans, oaks, and hardwoods. We arrived at Uncle Joe's Landing, the nearest access to the Mississippi River. As the truck angled up the steep side of the levee I caught a glimpse of Old Man River glinting broadly in the late afternoon sun. It was wide, beautifully strong with its backdrop of white, sun washed sand bars and green tree-lined sloughs.

Daddy parked the truck at the base of the levee and barked, "Grab your buckets. We'll get our blackberry picking done first and then you may play." The wild blackberry bushes, growing in tangles of underbrush along the banks of the Mississippi River, provided the sweetest of fruits. Sun-ripened, the rich blackberries were like candy and even better in Mama's blackberry pie whose homemade Crisco crust was carefully crimped, amply sprinkled on top with sugar, and marked with beautiful designs by the tines of a fork.

"Oh, Daddy, look," gasped Katy, her hair divided into two pigtails and tied at the ends with pink ribbons. "A long snake just went near my foot and I think it might be a water moccasin!"

"It's not going to bother you if you leave it alone," replied Daddy briskly as he efficiently pulled blackberries with both hands, ignoring the sticker pricks that were beginning to make his rough hands bleed. "Keep on picking. I've got my gun if we need it."

When the blackberry bushes were depleted, we walked down to the sand bar and poured over the driftwood and treasures that the River had deposited by its edge, making a pile of the driftwood to use later for our fire.

"Take off your shoes," Margot insisted, looking at our feet in white sneakers purchased from Sears. "Let's make witches brew." All five of us tread up and down on the sand bar, much like Italians pressing juice out of grapes, and soon we felt the cold Mississippi River ooze through the sand between our toes. We pretended the mixture was quicksand, a witch's brew. We sank lower and lower into the sand pits, imagining we were being dragged away, never to return home again, to Sheol where witches wickedly stirred their foaming poison pots.

"Don't get too close to the water's edge, kids," sternly warned Daddy. We knew about the swirling, deadly whirlpools of the mighty Mississippi and how the strongest swimmer could easily be pulled under to his death in a moment's time. We watched spellbound as large logs floating recklessly down the river were sucked like matchsticks into unsuspecting whirlpools, disappearing into a breathless, bottomless hole and never reappearing.

A large barge loaded with grain heading south to New Orleans appeared around the bend of the river. "Crook your arm and signal the captain in the tugboat!" shouted Stephan. We all crooked our arms, moved them up and down in a time worn signal to the tugboat captain. He obliged and sent a deep throated whistle that echoed loudly from side to side of the wide river channel.

Stephan grinned proudly, "See! I told you! Keep it up!"

"I have cardboard in the bed of the truck," Daddy yelled. That meant one thing. We could slide down the steep sides of the levee using the cardboard as our sleds. We scrambled to the truck, each of us grabbing a flattened cardboard box and made our way to the top of the levee. Lining up in a row we jumped on our cardboard sleds, snowboarding over the tall summer grass and mounds of sweet clover, trying to be the first to the bottom of the hill. Stephan usually claimed that honor. He would ride down, one knee up with the other leg bracing his sled, adeptly steering while using his weight for momentum. The rest of us reached bottom in a mangled heap of laughter eager to make the long trek up the levee again for a repeat ride and a possible first place victory.

Soon the weary sun began to dip low casting an orange glow over the River and Daddy started a fire using the sun dried, crisp driftwood. We skewered hot dogs on coat hangers over the driftwood coals, often burning the exterior and finding the interior of the meat still cold. We found them delicious. We feasted on Mama's baked beans sweetened with ample brown sugar and slow baked in the oven, her potato salad made from potatoes peeled carefully by her small utility knife, stuffed eggs, and juicy sliced tomatoes, plucked from the tomato plants just that morning, still warm from the garden. Daddy cut open a fresh watermelon with his pocket knife and we finished the meal slow roasting our marshmallows over the dying coals. Sometimes a marshmallow enveloped in flames and turned instantly black. Katy would giggle. Daddy ate the burned marshmallows anyway. There would be no wasting of good food.

As dark fell and stars crisscrossed the blue dome sky, Daddy said, "Hey, kids, let's head up to the top of the levee before we leave." Mama spread Grandma's wedding ring quilt for all seven of us to pile upon.

"Who can find Orion, the Hunter?" Daddy queried. It was his favorite constellation; hunting was his passion.

"There it is." Stephan quickly exclaimed, pointing to the belt and the bow. We also found our other favorites – the North Star, the Big and Little Dippers spilling their milk across the Milky Way, the Bear, and Cassiopeia.

"Look, a shooting star!" Stephan exclaimed pointing to the east. A quick burst of flame had seared the sky, fizzling like a Fourth of July rocket, disappearing into nothingness.

"Quick, everyone make a wish," Margot insisted. We squeezed our eyes shut and thought of the happiest wish we each could imagine. I wanted a bike.

Abruptly, Daddy stood up. "Load up. Time to go." He moved briskly toward the truck and we followed, piling into the back, slumping against the truck bed walls. Driving home under the canopy of the night, the cool nighttime breeze sweeping over our tired bodies, we heard through the open truck windows Mama's soft singing:

"Old Man River, that Old Man River

He don't know nothin', but he must know somethin'

That Old Man River, he just keep a'rollin' along.

He don't plant taters,

He don't pick cotton,

But them that plants 'em, are soon forgotten,

That Old Man River, he just keeps a'rollin' along."

The Lord's Day

It was always a day set apart. The Lord's Day. My parents firmly believed the biblical account. Six days shalt thou labor. On the seventh day thou shalt rest. Remember the Sabbath day to keep it holy.

We began preparing several days before. Reatta, the maid, starched and pressed the family's cotton dresses, pants, shirts, and handkerchiefs on Friday and laid them out. It took a full morning. I had watched her set up the heavy black iron, mix the batch of starch, unroll the sprinkled clothes onto the kitchen table, then go and spit tobacco juice out the back door. I whispered to Stephan, "Why does Reatta spit black and we spit white?"

"Because she's mean," Stephan responded sullenly. Reatta would swat us with a switch from the backyard or with Mama's plastic flyswatter, but she especially had an eye for every slight misdemeanor in which Stephan might engage.

"Girls," Mama called each Saturday evening. "Come polish your shoes and then get your baths." We pulled our white patent leather shoes out of the closet, carefully spread the Greenville Delta Democrat Times newspaper over the hardwood floors, and proceeded to cover the black scuffs and scrapes that invariably appeared from week to week, the inevitable outcome of playing tag in the church yard.

"Now set the shoes near your dresses then lay out your Bibles, your white purses and gloves, get your tithe money, your

Sunday School books, and your pencils," Mama continued as she began preparing the Sunday pot roast. She placed a large portion of meat in the speckled blue roaster along with garden potatoes, carrots, and onion, ready to be popped into the oven early Sunday morning. Mama pulled her cherry and pecan pies, their homemade Crisco crusts a light golden brown, out of the oven and put into the refrigerator our favorite layered strawberry Jell-O made in a Tupperware ring mold. When unmolded, the middle had a center of sour cream. The yeast rolls were rolled out, rising in the warm summer kitchen.

    We bathed, making bubble baths from Joy detergent, and washed our long hair that reached to our waists, slipping into clean summer nightgowns and robes that Mama had sewn on her black Singer treadle sewing machine. Stephan and Dani were next, scrubbing the dirt and grime of a dusty Delta Saturday.

    Mama called, "Time for a story," and opened to a chapter of *Five Little Peppers and How They Grew*, as we stretched long on the braided living room rug, pillows under our heads. There were other favorites – *Cheaper by the Dozen*, *The House on Pooh Corner*. Mama combed the shelves of the Bolivar County bookmobile when it came weekly to the Delta Pine community. Her voice was soft and gentle and she altered her tones, assuming the role of each character. A former elementary school teacher, she delighted in opening the world of reading to our family.

    Sometimes Mama led us in our favorite repeat along story, *Going on a Lion Hunt*, complete with its hand clapping motions. We never tired of that one. As our eyes began to close, Daddy led in family prayers and we climbed into our bunk beds. Snuggled under sun dried sheets that had hung on the clothesline all day and carried the sweet smell of red summer clover, we fell to sleep listening to the throaty song of bullfrogs which formed a chorus line on the banks of Deer Creek.

Awaking early on Sunday morning, our family quickly ate a breakfast of Mama's homemade cinnamon rolls drizzled with icing accompanied by a glass of icy cold milk, dressed, and made beds. Daddy was never late and no one was allowed to make the family late.

"Load up," Daddy commanded at the exact precise minute we needed to depart. Dashing out the back screen door, we seven piled into the white family station wagon, bodies wriggling into assigned positions, each stashing Bibles, Sunday school books, pencils, and purses within reach. We drove the fifteen miles, windows rolled down for air, south on Highway One, the Old River Road, to Greenville where we worshipped. Mama was church pianist and sometimes organist and Daddy served as Sunday School Superintendent.

After driving the fifteen miles back home, we walked into a house filled with the delectable aroma of the pot roast meal. Following lunch, Mama issued the weekly reminder, "Rest time, children." We could read quietly on our beds for one hour, set by Mama on the oven kitchen timer, if we could not drop off to sleep. Sunday afternoon rest time was as non-negotiable as failing to set aside the Lord's Day for worship.

However, after the timer buzzed, we could play quietly as long as we did not disturb Mama and Daddy's nap.

On Saturday, Mama had made homemade play dough, a mixture of flour, oil, and salt, to which food coloring was added. There were balls of green and yellow play dough set out on the counter today in a green Tupperware bowl. "I'll get the wooden rolling pin and cookie cutters," Margot said as I prepared the kitchen table.

Katy and I made rows of ducks and gingerbread men, half moons and giraffes, Christmas trees and stars. Margot located the stash of construction paper, glue, crayons, and pens purchased at the Ben Franklin store on Main Street in Greenville and began making paper designs. The Lord's Day, tranquil under the heavy drone of the attic fan, slipped quietly by.

Upon waking from her nap, Mama appeared in the kitchen, tied her apron around her waist, and prepared to make a platter of homemade candy. Sometimes it was divinity, or chocolate fudge, or butterscotch, but today it was my favorite, homemade caramel. I watched her stir the cream, sugar, butter, and corn syrup in her big copper bottomed pot, waiting for the boiling mixture to turn from white to light caramel and finally to a dark caramel color.

"Anna Beth," Mama called as she vigorously stirred the boiling syrup. "Get me a cup of ice water so that we can test the candy." She dropped a bit of syrup inside the cold water to see if it would form a soft ball. Finally, it formed the perfect ball and Mama poured the candy onto her yellow candy platter.

Mama got five spoons, scraped the pan, and provided an early taste for each of us while the boiling hot caramel candy was left to cool.

In the late afternoon, we dressed again for church, ate a sandwich and leftovers for supper, and headed up Highway One to Greenville, once again. Night church was our favorite with its more relaxed worship, times of hymn singing and testimonies, and games of hide and seek in the dark church yard under a lone streetlight while the adults fellowshipped.

The ride home in the quiet summertime darkness was cloaked in peace; the cool night air and the smell of honeysuckle mixed with clover grass wafted through the open car windows. We listened to the rhythmic thud of the station wagon's tires as we traveled the lonely concrete road. Mama hummed quietly her favorite hymn, a nightingale tune in the dark:

"Great is Thy Faithfulness, O God my Father.

There is no shadow of turning with Thee.

Thou changest not, Thy compassions they fail not.

As Thou has been Thou forever wilt be."

We dozed, awakening as Daddy carried Katy and Dani to their bunk beds.

Silver Dollar Incentive

"Mama, is the swimming pool open yet?" asked Katy who tossed restlessly, moving from bow to stern on her bunk bed during noon rest time.

"No, it won't open until one o'clock; that's forty minutes from now. Go back to reading your library book," Mama called from the kitchen as she put away the last of lunch -- leftovers of fresh garden vegetables, venison, and peach cobbler with the crust that rises to the top in the oven.

The stove top timer arduously ticked away the weighty minutes of a mandatory one hour rest time before swim time. Margot and I read the Nancy Drew and Hardy Boy mysteries we had checked out from Bolivar County's traveling bookmobile. We cocked our ears, attentively, impatiently, willing the buzzer to sound. We were dressed in our skirted swim suits, our towels and terry cloth robes draped over the rungs of the beds, with our matching flip flops carefully positioned on the floor for a quick exit. The attic fan droned, moving the humid Mississippi air in welcome drafts about the beds. Temperatures on the late June Mississippi Delta noonday steadily climbed like the sun ball of fire positioned directly overhead, casting shimmer waves upon the street pavement.

Today was no ordinary pool day. It was the day Margot and I would try to earn our coveted silver dollars. Each child in the Delta Pine community who swam the length of the pool from shallow to deep end without touching either side received a silver dollar from the Delta Pine Bank.

We were nervous. Everyone would be watching. Patient and kind Mrs. Gray, the company president's gentle wife, had recently taught us to swim and we desperately wanted to be able to join the older kids playing water games of Marco Polo and sharks and minnows in the deep end. The silver dollar was a rites of passage obligation understood by the whole community as a requirement for deep end swimming privileges.

An eternity passed. The stove timer screeched. We had finally dozed on our bunks and awoke startled, scrambling to grab robes and scoot into flip-flops. We raced across the street and over the Deer Creek footbridge that led to the Delta Pine pool. Stephan won the foot race, as usual, jumping boisterously into the shallow end. Mama followed behind, strolling Dani who still slept, perspiration beginning to form around his head in the midday heat.

Margot and I deposited our belongings in a hurried heap on the concrete strip bordering the shallow end and jumped, hand in hand, into the pool together, our opposite hands holding our noses. We filled our lungs to the brim, began the maiden voyage, and determined to succeed without touching bottom or reaching for the sides. As we each reached the deep end wall, cheers erupted and Mama and Mrs. Gray beamed their approval from the shallow end.

We quickly donned our pink and yellow terry cloth robes and flip-flops and walked the two blocks to the Delta and Pine

Land Company Bank. Timidly, we explained our feat to Mr. Boyd, the spry bank director who peered kindly down at us over wire rimmed glasses. We waited expectantly at the bank window as he ducked into the massive bank vault.

I whispered to my sister, "I really think that millions of dollars are stacked on shelves in there, enough to operate all of Delta Pine. You know it's the largest cotton plantation in the world and that would take a lot of money, I imagine."

Reappearing with a huge grin, Mr. Boyd proudly presented each of us a heavy silver dollar. We fingered our treasure as though it were an Olympic gold medal and tucked them in our robe pockets. I would deposit mine later in my small, copper bank shaped like the Empire State Building. Mama and Daddy had brought me the bank following a trip they made into New York City when Daddy was studying for his doctorate at Cornell.

Leaving the Delta Pine office building we went next door to the Scott Drug Store, proudly purchased grape popsicles for a nickel, and slowly licked them on our triumphant walk along the edge of Deer Creek and back to the swimming pool, trying to guess on which side of the shark and minnow teams we would be placed by the older neighborhood swimmers.

Depot Downtown

"Girls, come inside, please," Mama called, poking her head quickly through the back screen door. "I need you to run some errands for me."

Margot and I hopped dizzily off our tire swing under the pecans and dashed through the back screen door, letting it slam with a bang. Errands sometimes meant sneaking upstairs in the Delta Pine Office building to Daddy's office and persuading him to buy us an icy cold ten cent coke cola from the squat coke machine downstairs, that is if Daddy was not over at the Cotton Research Department with his research seed and plant breeding projects.

Running errands often included taking Mama's list into Scott Store where a tempting stash of penny candy sat safely on the shelves behind Mr. Swilley, whose speedy fingers rang up the cost of each grocery item on the mammoth cash register. Behind him, neatly displayed in cardboard boxes were root beer barrels, pixie stick straws filled with sweet and sour powder, wax candy lips shaped in a smile, tootsie roll pops with soft chocolate centers, and bubble gum packs with baseball cards.

Mama pulled out her list, carefully copied in even, cursive, teacher handwriting on a piece of steno pad paper. "First, I need this letter mailed to Grandma and Grandpa in Palo Alto. We'll be taking a trip to see them in California in a few weeks and I want to make sure they know the dates of our expected arrival. Then, I'll need you to take this sack lunch to

Daddy at the office; he can't stop to come home for lunch today. Next, go by Scott Store for some food items and dry goods. They are all on the list here. Thank you, girls. Be back in time for lunch."

Margot deposited the list in her dress pocket and we ran to our rooms to scrounge for two nickels. We walked toward downtown, past the LeLeux's house next door, past the corner vacant lot at the end of the residential street where we congregated regularly with our neighborhood friends for sand-lot football, baseball, dodge ball, and tag, and night time hide and go seek.

At the back of the vacant lot sat the small telephone switchboard office for the Delta Pine community manned by Mrs. Turbeville, the operator. Perched in front of a large picture window with headset intact, Mrs. Turberville sat next to a large switchboard with its myriad of wires and cords. She manually connected calls to homes and Delta Pine offices. From this prized vantage point, Mrs. Turbeville gained great insight into all the comings and goings of the Delta Pine community. Grandma often laughed when she called from California. "No," Mrs. Turbeville would say to Grandma's request to be connected to our home telephone, "Elinor's not at home. She just left for Scott Store. She'll probably be back home within thirty minutes. Ya'll call back then, ya' hear!"

We crossed the street from the vacant lot over to the Scott Post Office, located in the grey weathered Scott Train Depot station that stood beside the railroad tracks. Trains passed regularly through downtown, picking up loads of cotton bales, cotton seed, soybeans, rice, sorghum, and other Delta Pine products for their destinations southbound to New Orleans or northbound to Memphis. Sometimes, when no train was in sight, we would slip a coin on the tracks to flatten it and we would return later to retrieve our flattened treasure. Not today. There were no coins we cared to spare.

Entering the post office depot, clean and tidy with its rows of mail boxes on the walls, Margot spoke to stern, spry Mrs. Hatcher behind the iron barred window. "May I please have five stamps?" Margot asked timidly, handing the tight-lipped postmistress a quarter.

Mrs. Hatcher's face softened and she replied, "Why good morning Margot and Anna Beth. We got in some new ones with the New York World's Fair on them. Look, see how nice they look."

We both nodded politely and Margot carefully licked one of the five cent stamps for Grandma and Grandpa's letter, passing it through the drop box, depositing the remaining four stamps in her skirt pocket.

From the Post Office, we walked past Scott Store, the Scott Drug Store, and down to the Delta Pine Business Office where Daddy's office sat overlooking Deer Creek. We quietly climbed the stairs to his office in the corner where piles of field log books, numerous papers marked with statistical calculations, books intermingled with current plant breeding journals, and a large desk calculating machine with rows of numbers covered his massive wooden desk. We quickly deposited the sack lunch and scurried, like squirrels chasing one another in the tree branches, down the stairs.

Looking at the grocery list as we turned back toward town, Margot remarked, "We only need to pick up bread, milk, a package of hot dogs and buns, and some spools of thread and a few other sewing items for Mama's sewing project."

"Good," I replied. "We'll have plenty of time to figure out the candy we want to buy."

We entered Scott Store with its clean wooden plank floors and went over to the dry goods department located in an alcove at the right side of the store. Mrs. Davenport, dressed smartly in a fashionable tweed suit, hair coiffed neatly, called, "Mornin' girls. What can I get for you?"

I replied, "Mama's sewing today and needs some thread to match these pieces of fabric," handing her two small scraps of flannel material that would be made into soft nightgowns, pink for the girls, and navy pajamas for the boys.

"I'll fix you right up, girls. Go finish your shopping and pick this up on the way out. I'll just put it on your Dad's ticket," continued Mrs. Davenport moving to select the thread from a large, mahogany spool cabinet containing a series of drawers, set upon on the front glass counter. "Mind, tell your Mama, I've been to Memphis shopping and think I've found a pretty dress for your Mama."

"Yes, Ma'am," we replied turning to the grocery section to pick up the items on Mama's list.

"This goes on your Dad's ticket, right?" asked Mr. Swilley as he swiftly rang up the food items.

"Yes, sir," said Margot, "but we want to buy some candy with our own money."

"Sure," the storekeeper smiled knowingly. "Come round here, pick it out, and we'll put it into separate little brown paper sacks for you."

Heading home with dry goods wrapped in brown paper tied with strings and groceries in brown paper bags, we saw our friends gathering on the corner lot for dodge ball. "Go get Stephan and come back to play," hollered Kirby. "We need everyone we can find today."

"Sure, we'll ask Mama but I know we can't come until we eat lunch," said Margot.

We entered the house and saw Mama boiling fresh ears of sweet corn picked by Daddy early that morning. A chocolate sheet cake laden with chocolate pecan icing sat cooling on the counter next to the pitcher of freshly made sweet tea. "Got everything, girls? Thank you so much. Now, mind you, I hope you didn't eat any candy before lunch. It will spoil your appetite for good food." But she had turned back to stir the ears of corn before she could see us blush.

Westward Bound

We loaded the station wagon with our suitcases the night before, each sibling getting half a suitcase for our clothes with Dani's clothes going into Mama and Daddy's bigger suitcase. We laid beside our beds our travel clothes, a light sweater, and our small bags of reading books, paper and pens, small toys, anything we could think of to break the monotony of the long road trip ahead to see Grandma and Grandpa in California. Excitement made it hard to sleep.

"Load up." Daddy's sharp command shattered our sleep and the clock's groggy hands pointed to an incredulous 4:00 a.m. Daddy believed it important to make time on the road early while the rest of the world slept, particularly with a station wagon load of young children. In a sleepwalk stupor, we slipped on our clothes, grabbed our pillows and entertainment bags and piled into the car. Our summer trip was finally here. As Daddy backed quietly out of the driveway, the gravel crunching, I turned to look at our dark home and realized Daddy had not even locked the front door. We never locked the doors, not even when we left on a three week trip.

I longed to stay awake and see the bridge as we crossed the Mississippi River from Mississippi into Arkansas. I could see Orion the Hunter from my window, our angel guardian in constellation disguise, and smelled the fruity odor of acres of flooded rice fields, their green stalks growing Delta strong.

Somewhere along Old River Road, as our car tires thudded, patiently treading mile upon mile, I dozed, my feather pillow pressed against Margot's.

The car stopped. The sun was now in full morning bloom and Daddy had pulled into a restaurant for breakfast, exiting to stretch his weary lower back. How could four hours in the station wagon have passed so quickly? We rolled out, stiff from embryonic sleeping positions, our mole eyes blinking through Chinese slivers.

"What kind of pancake syrup are you going to get, Margot?" I asked my sister.

"Probably blueberry," she responded, "How about you?"

"I might try the raspberry this time," I replied. We were amazed at the number of different types of pancake syrup displayed in an array of glass, silver tipped jars. Boysenberry, strawberry, pecan, maple, blackberry, peach. Never had pancake breakfast choices been so delectably varied and we savored each sticky bite.

The adventure had begun. Getting back into the station wagon, we pulled out books, paper pads, played road sign games, took turns riding up front between Mama and Daddy with the primary privilege of finding a radio station. Before long, it was noon and our stomachs, once crammed with syrup sopped pancakes and crisp bacon slices, were now empty. Daddy found a grocery store in a small west Louisiana town and we went inside to purchase sandwich makings, fruit, and milk. On our summer road trips we were allowed to buy fruit that normally was too expensive for the weekly shopping trips and today we picked fresh Bing cherries.

After getting back on the road, Daddy announced, "Whoever can first spot the next roadside park for lunch will get a quarter." That was great incentive. We were attentive, focused on the challenge and not our restless legs and rumbling stomachs. Up ahead a park appeared with its covered concrete table and benches surrounded by grassy knolls. "Zip," Stephan shouted. "There it is." Zip was the traveling word game we used when Daddy challenged us to spot the owls on the telephone lines looking for mouse prey, or the horses in the pasture, or any other random creature of his choice.

Following lunch, we played tag and chased the travel stiffness out of our bones. This was only day one of our trip to California but Daddy's travel system was a good one and by three or four in the afternoon we reached the appointed stop on our route, a designated Holiday Inn with a swimming pool. Daddy and Mama fell into their beds for a late afternoon nap while we scattered to fill ice buckets, ride the elevator up and down, explore the property, and wait for swim time when Daddy and Mama awoke.

After a supper of hamburger and French fries at the Holiday Inn, Daddy announced, "Eight o'clock, kids. Bedtime. Wake-up is at four."

"Make sure your clothes are laid out," Mama added.

"Yes, Ma'am," we replied crawling contentedly under crisp, steam roller pressed cotton hotel sheets.

Dani was overtired and fretful. We fell asleep listening as Mama sang to him:

"Fly away Kentucky babe, fly away and rest.

Sleep Kentucky babe. Lay yo' little wooly head on yo' Mammy's breast.

Sleep Kentucky babe.

Sandman am a comin' for to take this boy of mine.

You is mighty lucky. Babe of ole' Kentucky.

Close yo' eyes and sleep. Sleep. Sleep."

Grandma's Pink House

The journey west had not been as the crow flies. Daddy had cotton research plots in Lubbock, Texas and we dipped south to allow time for him to gather research data. We tried to be patient as he walked the dusty cotton rows, pencil and log book in hand, assessing the grade, color, strength of the new cotton variety he was in the process of developing. We sought shade at the edge of the turn rows, but the morning sun beat us into sullen submission. There was a reward for patience, though. Daddy promised ice cream bars and candy at the next filling station.

We piled out of the station wagon, dust covered and sweaty, at the Esso gas station near Lubbock and the young gas attendant came to fill the station wagon with thirty cent gasoline. He thoroughly washed the south Texas grime off the front window. Inside, we selected our treats, reveling in the cool reprieve of the dark gas station where a rotating metal fan desperately chased the oppressive hot air out the front door. My eyes caught a tangled mass of tumbleweed as it dashed against the gas pump then rebound the opposite direction like a drunken man tottering toward town.

Daddy broke up the long journey, now up Route 66 Westward, by introducing us to great American landmarks along the way. We visited the Grand Canyon, painted with God's giant paintbrush, and Carlsbad Caverns with its night flying bats and terrifying dark when its lights were turned off. Then there was a wee early, tense morning drive across desolate Death Valley Desert, where we prayed the station wagon would not overheat, and where we passed not a single vehicle.

By the time we reached Palo Alto, however, there was no more welcome sight than Grandma's pink cottage home. It sat, a picture postcard, framed with roses, her backyard filled with flowers juxtaposed against small, airy houses for the baby canaries she raised to sell. We raced toward the front door into the arms of red-headed Grandma and tall, straight backed, stately Grandpa. Mama had told me that all of Grandma's young life she had been told as a red headed girl, she simply could not wear pink. Throwing off the rigid color taboo, she now surrounded herself with pink, to include her pink home, her pink roses, and her pink flowered summer dress. She was a beautiful sight.

We were also greeted by Grandma's two Pomeranian dogs with coats the exact color of Grandma's hair and her talking parrot who could sing Happy Birthday. It felt so good to sit, though we continued to feel the endless driving motion of the station wagon in our bodies much like an amputee senses the presence of a limb no longer there.

Grandpa had planned wonderful day trips. He drove us along the exquisite Palisades highway to reach the Pacific

Ocean. We were shocked to see its huge waves, feel the cold whip of the wind around our faces, and catch our breaths when the ocean's icy teeth bit our bare feet pushing us angrily away from its edge. Our only beach reference was the Gulf of New Mexico, which by July felt like a warm bathtub, and we learned that even building a sand castle left us bone-chilled, teeth chattering, our cotton white sweaters wind snatched.

Grandpa found us a warm café afterward for hot chocolate and cheese toast sandwiches where we talked about the marvel of the huge, dark waves and the surfers who sailed for hundreds of yards, balanced fearlessly, like Greek gods on their pedestals.

On our visit to San Francisco, we discovered the Golden Gate Bridge was not golden. Its red rusted exterior was a huge disappointment, but the massive expanse of the city of San Francisco stretching with great majesty on its opposite side, towering over the Pacific Ocean seashore, put us in awe. Our favorite place was China Town and Grandpa wove skillfully in and out of traffic to our amazement. "We have the coolest Grandfather," Margot said quietly to me. "How many Grandfathers can drive in a city like this?" We squealed as Grandpa took us down the most crooked street in the world.

Yosemite Park opened a world of beauty to us we had never seen – the Bridal Falls Waterfall, rushing streams, the Half Dome towering in the mountain peaks. Breathtaking, marvelous beauty. We ate a picnic lunch prepared by Grandma and climbed and played like colts, basking in the brisk mountain air, sun chilled and free.

At Stanford University Grandpa took us by the location of the atom-smasher and tried to explain the energy implications as a result of the ability to split atoms. Much, though it went over our heads, we recalled in later years as we studied Einstein and scientific principles and we thought of Grandpa's patient explanations.

All too soon, our summer visit was over and we hugged tearful goodbyes with precious grandparents who had expanded our worlds and poured love and time into our lives. "Our turn," next summer, "Grandma said. "We'll bring our travel trailer and head Mississippi way, but we'll need to come before it gets too hot."

We waved at the two figures, standing hand in hand, in front of the pink cottage, and snuggled into our assigned positions in the station wagon, resigned to begin our long journey back to the Mississippi Delta but secretly eager return to our own sweet home once again.

Fourth of July

　　Summer solstice had passed, unnoticed, as we crossed the days off the kitchen calendar, one by one, until we reached a starred and circled date, the Fourth of July. It would seem an eternity as we awaited our trip to Greenville for the anticipated community fireworks celebration on the levee overlooking the Mississippi River. Mama baked bread for the night picnic supper which included roast beef sandwiches, slices of chilled watermelon and tomato from the garden, potato chips, bottles of coke cola and a hand-churned batch of vanilla ice cream, the bucket carefully iced down and covered in newspapers and blankets to harden, protected from the rising Mississippi heat.

　　Our afternoon swim was shortened, allowing us to come home and wash and braid our long hair, slip into freshly starched dresses, and help Mama clean the house and load the car. The sun refused to set. It lingered stubbornly at the horizon as though commanded by Joshua of old to skip a day in time. Daddy insisted the fireworks would not begin until well after sun set and there was no point in sitting on the levee swatting mosquitoes for hours waiting on the fireworks show to begin.

　　"Load up," came the long anticipated command from Daddy. We rolled our car windows down waging combat with the evening July heat bombs pummeling our skin and chatted about what this year's fireworks show would look like.

Mama suggested, "Let's stop at Shipley's donuts and pick up some cream filled horns to add to our celebration picnic supper." Daddy agreed and rerouted to the bakery, finally pulling up at the bottom of the Greenville levee giving orders on how we were to carry our picnic loads up the levee side. We found neighbors and church family already there and joined the throngs assembling on the levee top.

The levee was a huge mosaic, a patchwork quilt of blankets, picnic baskets and wrapped ice cream buckets. A buzz of wriggling children bodies dashed to and fro like bees making honey, the assembly stretching like a linked chain for hundreds of yards. The orange fire ball finely set, plummeting with a resigned sigh to the lonely, dark bottom of the muddy Mississippi River. We watched a tug boat as it pushed from shore and positioned itself in the middle of the river, serving as the launching point for the fireworks. We could see the red glow of the fireworks lighting stick.

We waited, impatiently, looking up at the navy star dome and finding Orion. "The '27 Break, kids," Daddy began, filling time with a history lesson, "happened in the Mississippi Delta about halfway between here and Uncle Joe's Landing, at Mounds Landing, across from the Winterville Indian mounds." We knew this story, but loved to hear it retold. We often rode the levee from Scott all the way to Greenville.

"That was back when the levees were not built as high or as solid as these levees," Daddy continued. "In April of 1927, the levee broke at Mounds Landing. Four hundred fifty men worked through the night stacking sand bags to repair the levee, but the river rose too quickly. Fifteen hundred additional men were rushed to the site in the early morning, but Old Man River would not be stopped. Every church bell, mill whistle, and fire whistle sounded warning the residents. One hundred eighty five thousand people were forced to evacuate as the River flooded the Mississippi Delta fifty miles to the east and almost one hundred miles to the South. Even as far as Yazoo City, the water rose high enough to cover roof tops. Never before had a levee break been so severe and the Mississippi Delta land became an ocean."

The first fireworks now spewed and sputtered shakily into the sky as Daddy's history lesson rang in our ears. I looked at the Mississippi river, sluggish, hot, and tired on this July Fourth night. It seemed impossible for me to picture it raging, foaming, gnashing its levee boundaries over like a massive bulldozer set on reconstructing its own pathway. A welcome night breeze stirred off its waters, winding its way up the levee side and weaving like fluttering angel's wings among the expectant crowds.

"I think the next firework will be a spidery one that is green and blue that will fizzle at its tail," Margot said to me. We tried to guess the size, color, and shape of each magical explosion that lit up the dark wonder sky. Soon, it was over. The tugboat shot a rapid volley of color upon color, a kaleidoscope about which we would dream that night.

We gathered blankets, picnic supplies, and ran down the levee to our station wagon, finishing the sweet crème horns on the way home. The car was quiet. Dani slept up front. Mama sang quietly and the words floated through open windows:

> "Somewhere over the rainbow, way up high
> There's a land that I've heard of once in a lullaby.
> Somewhere over the rainbow, skies are blue
> And the dreams that you dare to dream
> Really do come true.
>
> Someday I'll wish upon a star
> And wake up where the clouds are far behind me.
> Where troubles melt like lemon drops,
> High above the chimney tops,
> That's where you'll find me.
>
> Somewhere over the rainbow, blue birds fly
> Birds fly over the rainbow
> Why then, oh why can't I?
> If happy little bluebirds fly beyond the rainbow
> Why, oh why can't I?"

Every time I heard Mama sing that song it stirred up memories of brilliant Mississippi Delta rainbows after violent summer thunderstorms. I could see in my mind's eye a huge pot spilling gold pieces and a black cauldron over whose edges candy of all shapes and sizes flowed. Both glimmered in the rain-soaked cotton fields just below the rainbow's arch, a reachable distance, waiting for our family to come and claim.

Field Days

We grew up hearing that Delta Pine was famous for being the world's largest plantation and we swelled with pride. Some challenged that claim but the challenge never rattled our confidence or assurance of such. The operation in its prime spread over 37,700 acres with 25,000 acres in cropland and the remainder in cattle, woodlands, and for other uses. Cotton, soybeans, and rice were the crops primarily grown for sale and for seed production. Farming operations included sixteen plantation units as well as the research farm for the development of improved seed varieties. We also knew Delta Pine was owned by the British manufacturer, Fine Cotton Spinners and Doubler's Association, LTD, but there was rumor the company would be sold to Courtaulds, another British fiber manufacturing operation. We envisioned lords and ladies, massive cotton spinning mills, visits by the Queen to their manufacturing dynasties. The whole notion was romantic, threads of our lives in the Mississippi Delta tied to Europe and our mother country, England.

Because of Delta Pine's unique setting and its stature in the seed production business, planters, farmers, and businessmen came from around the world to learn about the company's newest seed varieties and its farming techniques. Near the end of summer the whole Delta Pine community prepared for Field Days. Plantation managers tidied up their turn-rows ensured stray weeds were plucked from the endless acres of immaculate crops. The Delta Pine Research Farm created large signs on stakes naming each cotton and soybean variety, the stakes pounded into the fertile Delta soil in front of each test plot. The town manicured its lawns, tended its flowers, and weeded its gardens.

Central hub was the Scott Community Center, positioned near the office buildings, Scott store, drug store, and the gins. Plantation managers drove a few of their tractors to town, attaching wagons lined with hay bales, in which guests would ride to the various field sites. The green cotton fields now flowered, white and purple, a promise of milky white cotton bolls to come in some week's time. Cooks prepared the kitchen at the community center. They fried chicken, fish, and hushpuppies, baked biscuits and brownies, iced down coca colas and ice cream sandwiches. The whole community could sense the anticipation, the privilege of swarms of guest visiting, marveling at the agricultural wonder which was Delta Pine.

Mama gave us the same community warning given to all the Delta Pine children, "You must stay out of the way and not be underfoot. You may not go to the community center or even to downtown Scott without my permission. We will play in our yards and still go swimming each afternoon. No loud noise, no rambunctious running about."

We sighed. "But," Mama continued, "Remember, the final day of field days, the families get to participate, go on the field tours, and eat the chicken lunch." That would make it all worthwhile and we knew we could do all she had said for the privilege ahead.

Mama dressed us in starched cotton dresses and starched shirts each day of the field days and we watched the stream of visitors pour up and down the street in front of Deer Creek. We played ping-pong on our front porch, giving us a bird's eye, yet legal, view of the community center activities directly across the street. We climbed the magnolia tree to see further up and down the road.

After a day or two, we became bored and asked Mama, "May we play up in the attic today?"

"It's pretty hot up there, but you can try." Mama responded. We pulled down the ladder leading to the attic and carried up our Monopoly game to play bank, our own game with our own rules. We took up our Barbie dolls and dressed them and played hairdresser with one another's hair. When it got too hot, we ventured down the ladder stairs for homemade lemonade popsicles frozen in Tupperware molds.

When the last day of field days arrived, the Delta Pine families met at the community center, fished iced down bottled coca colas from huge barrels, hopped aboard the tractor trailers, squeezing onto the bales of hay used as seating. We traveled to Daddy's research plot and learned about the latest seed variety in production, the Deltapine 16. Afterward, the tractor trailer took us to a plantation unit nearby and we listened to discussions about the new fertilizers and the airplane spraying techniques that helped deter the boll weevil and other pests.

Following the field tours, we were deposited at the community center for our fried chicken lunch and sat with our neighbors talking about the many people who had traveled long distances to come to our little town. A sense of relief flooded the community. We were no longer under careful scrutiny; we could return to racing about, life taking on its normal routine. Mama said to the neighborhood Moms, "Let's all meet at the pool at 2:00 today. We'll bring a few extra ice cream sandwiches home and take them over to snack on and we'll stay until closing time."

Summer's End

We were bored. Field days were over. The swimming pool had been drained and cleaned. The sweltering August heat kept us from playing neighborhood sand lot games until well after the sun had set and then it was time for bedtime. The garden stood stripped, dry, and bare save for melons which lay hidden among dry vines. We had read all the books in which we were interested on the shelves of the Bolivar County Bookmobile and we had poured over the gravel in our driveway and found every fossil and geode that could be found, storing them in a Mason jar.

After supper, Mama said, "Get your baths, kids, put on your robes, then we're going to learn some new games. This one is called Battleship." She brought out pencils and paper and showed us how to draw grids, letters across the top, numbers down the sides, and how to place our battleships in secret positions on the grids. This game interested us immensely, particularly Stephan. We spread out across the braided living room rug and reveled in sinking one another's warships as the stove timer ticked until bedtime.

"Bedtime," Daddy called.

"Tomorrow," Mama interjected, "is school shopping day. We're only a few days away from the first day of school, the day after Labor Day, so we need to get our shopping done."

Shopping day began early as we raced to beat the rising heat, arriving at Sears in Greenville as it opened. The shopping list noted new shoes and socks and Mama was going to look at some clothing. She had been sewing all summer, but the boys needed jeans and patches for those jeans, and she needed to make sure the Sears and Roebuck Christmas catalog would be sent to our address. Thirsty, we searched for the water fountains and saw two side by side, one marked Coloreds and one marked Whites. From Sears we went to Ben Franklin's Five and Dime Store for pencils, crayons, and notebooks, coloring books, and dot to dot books. We quickly tired of shopping.

"I've packed a lunch, children," Mama began, watching our fidgety summer browned bodies chaff at the constriction of confined city shopping. It was mid morning by now. "We'll stop by Shipley's Donuts, you may each pick a flavor, then head to the Greenville levee and you can race up and down after we eat an early lunch." We squealed. There were few things more delightful than racing up the levee and rolling like a torpedo down to its bottom.

Soon, hot and sweaty, grass covered, we eagerly climbed back into the station wagon, leaned our heads and arms out windows to cool off. "We'll set up the water sprinkler in the backyard; you can put on your bathing suits, and can cool down when we get home. I'll also make bubbles from Joy detergent for your bubble wands. Remember, we picked up some balloons at Ben Franklin's and you can make water bombs. Just don't throw them at one another's faces, please. Then we'll climb on our beds and finish the books that need to be returned to the book mobile this week. This will be its last run for the summer."

The attic fan droned, faithfully, powerfully, whipping the hot air up into our attic and sweeping us with pleasant drafts to cool the August mid afternoon as we rested. We thought about school. The bus would pick us up next door at the LeLeux's front yard. We would ride the five miles to Benoit Elementary School, north along Lake Bolivar, its curving banks edged with massive grey cypress trees, tall druids in rough monk clothing. I could see the huge oak tree at the elementary school under which Margot and I had played house and "Mary and Carol" for several school years.

I would have Mrs. Causey as a teacher this year and I was glad. She was grey haired, kind and she loved books, as did I. Margot had told me she let students read books when they finished their assigned paper work for each subject rather than have to sit, mind numbingly, waiting on the other students to finish. My mind flitted to earlier teachers. Mrs. Hogue taught us all first grade and she rewarded her readers with pieces of candy corn. I could see and taste that delicious candy corn now and would read anything she assigned just to get that piece of candy corn. The pictures in my readers were etched permanently upon my mind.

As I felt myself slipping into dreamland, I remembered my kindergarten year. We were still in New York, in Ithaca with its steep hills snow draped much of the winter. Daddy was finishing his doctoral thesis at Cornell in plant breeding and genetics. I attended the kindergarten on the Cornell campus and my school room was a miniature world: kitchen and all its equipment, blocks abundant, a real world brought to a tiny, magical size. I loved to go each afternoon, walking after lunch with my sister. In the evenings at home, Mama typed, long into the night, on thin, onion skinned paper interlaced with carbon paper, Daddy's complicated doctoral research thesis paper. Tap, tap, tap, return, tap, tap, tap. Memories, swirling, fading, dissolving. In my dreams I could see Orion continuing his eternal hunt through the night sky, a silent watcher over the house, the fields, even Old Man River himself. Yes, it would be a good school year and I was ready for it to begin.

Made in the USA
Columbia, SC
03 August 2022